Social Anxiety Workbook

By Logan Thomas

For more great books, visit:

EffingoPublishing.com

Download another book for Free

We want to thank you for purchasing this book and offer you another book (just as long and valuable as this book), "Health & Fitness Mistakes You Don't Know You're Making," completely free.

Visit the link below to signup and receive it:

www.effingopublishing.com/gift

In this book, we will break down the most common health & fitness mistakes, you are probably committing right now, and will reveal how you can quickly get in the best shape of your life!

In addition to this valuable gift, you will also have an opportunity to get our new books for free, enter giveaways, and receive other useful emails from us. Again, visit the link to sign up:

www.effingopublishing.com/gift

TABLE OF CONTENTS

Introduction 4

Chapter 1: You aren't alone – social Anxiety Strikes Again 6

Chapter 2: Breaking it down 18

Chapter 3: WHAT IS YOUR THOUGHT PATTERN? 30

Chapter 4: When and Where Does Social Anxiety Strike 38

Chapter 5: Action Plan 45

Chapter 6: Saying Bye To Your Fears And Hello To a New Life 60

Chapter 7: Rewire your anxious brain 70

Conclusion 100

Final Words 106

About the Co-Authors 107

Introduction

You are not alone. Don't let anxiety tell you otherwise. You are not alone.

Let us help you meet people and take you through experiences to help you understand what exactly anxiety is and what it does to us. This book covers anxiety in its every form and describes the medical, social, and emotional factors behind it. It also carries various solutions, including a complete guide to how to treat anxiety, diet plans, yoga exercise, and a surprise in the end!

Also, before you get started, I recommend you joining our email newsletter to receive updates on any upcoming new book releases or promotions. You can sign-up for free, and as a bonus, you will receive a gift. Our "*Health & Fitness Mistakes You Don't Know You're Making*" book! This book has been written to demystify, expose the top do's and don'ts and to finally equip you with the information you need to get in the best shape of your life. Due to the overwhelming amount of misinformation and lies told by magazines and self-proclaimed "gurus," it's becoming harder and harder to get reliable information to get in shape. As opposed to having to go through dozens of biased, unreliable, and untrustworthy sources to get your health & fitness information. Everything you need to help you has been broken down in this book for you to follow quickly and to immediately get results to achieve your desired fitness goals in the shortest amount of time.

Once again, to join our free email newsletter and to receive a free copy of this valuable book, please visit the link and signup now:

CHAPTER 1: YOU AREN'T ALONE – SOCIAL ANXIETY STRIKES AGAIN

When you're suffering from anxiety, "normal" is probably one of the last things you'd use to describe when you are talking about your experience. But this mental health disorder is more common than you think, and the feelings associated with it come from a deep-seated, primal within us.

One of your brain's primary functions is to keep you safe. It does this in uncountable ways you don't even pay attention to. For example, as you're reading this, your eyes are sending information to your visual system, which helps you learn and understand these words. At the same time, you're unconsciously scanning your surroundings for signs of danger. That's why sudden movements in the corners of your vision can capture your attention even if you're focusing on something else.

Similarly, your auditory system is listening not only for your phone ringing but also for crashes, bangs, and other sounds that could mean a hazard is nearby. Usually, these underlying functions of your brain serve to keep you aware of your environment, alerting you only when you should take action to protect yourself.

Sometimes, though, your brain chemistry reacts in a big way to a small event or no event at all, sending your heart into turmoil, making it beat fast and getting your body ready to fight or flee. These feelings of nervousness at the wrong times can be very uncomfortable, but they're also very common. Nearly 30 percent of people experience anxiety at some point in their lives.

It can be triggered anywhere. It can happen in a social situation, such as when you're delivering a speech or in a crowded room – this is classified as social anxiety. Sometimes, it happens suddenly when you are scared – this is defined as panic disorder. Other times, the excessive anxiousness people feel is simply tension, irritability, fatigue, and a feeling of being out-of-control that usually results in insomnia. All these disorders happen for the same reason. The brain's system for keeping us safe is in overdrive.

It's important to understand that brain chemistry is at all. The cycle of fear without reason often begins without warning and goes on without our input. Even if the feeling is triggered by an event, no one can give themselves an anxiety disorder, and no one should be expected to make it go away without some well-deserved assistance. That assistance can come in several forms – from therapy to mindfulness, to medication.

While transient feelings of nervousness can be a regular part of a healthy life, anxiety that persists for months with frequent, severe symptoms can make life harder and less comfortable than it should be. If you or someone you care about is suffering from regular anxiety, severe symptoms can make life harder and less uncomfortable than it should be. If you care about is suffering from frequent anxiety, talk to your health care provider. You're not alone, either in suffering or in deserving assistance. In time and with help, your brain will be able to resume its regular role as the primary protector of your well-being.

- From a high school student:

"When I was a freshman in high school, I had my first ever anxiety attack. I remember it was a Tuesday, right at the end of first-period biology class. I faked sick that day, told my teacher I needed to go home. I had no idea what was going on or how to handle the way my body was acting. This happened to me the next day and then the same thing the next two days after that until my mom suggested I see a doctor. They told me I had something called generalized social anxiety.

Little did I know what this was at the time, I ended up dealing with anxiety for the rest of high school, where it then followed me to college. I was such an outgoing, high energy goal-oriented individual at heart, but dealing with what was going on in my head held me back from all that for a long time. It took me years to see that I could be happy and continue moving forward while coping with anxiety. I ended up meeting so many different people while I was in college, while I traveled throughout Europe, dealing with different problems that were causing anxiety. For a long time, I went to therapy, I also tried medicine, and it all helped a little bit. But what I found helped me the most was surrounding myself with good people and then finding outlets in life to let this anxiety out, to express the way I was feeling in a new way. For me, that ended up being making videos. I started spending hours on these videos, and eventually, I was able to show my true self and let loose while making them. I started to see that, and that's when I realized I needed to share that on YouTube.

I saw that we were all in this together, all dealing with our problems either mentally or the challenges life throws at us.... I realized I wasn't alone. This right here is what made me want to speak out and create a video explaining my story; to tell people that they are not alone and the greatest thing we can do to show that is to express our stories, how we feel, and support one another. I have learned that anxiety never completely goes away, that it's more on a scale from 1- 10. The question is how we can keep that number as low as possible, find ways to be happy, and be at our best while chasing after our goals and dreams in life without being held back. The first step for me was to know that I had the right people in my life, and from there, I was able to take strong steps forward".

- From a college student

"Anxiety was hard for me because I couldn't differentiate between actual awful treatment from people and my horrible thoughts.

If someone were rude to me, I would think that it was my fault for overthinking the situation, so I would never say how

I felt when I was upset with the treatment I got from a friend or family member. It's hard to stand up for yourself when you have thoughts that make you doubt yourself all the time.

Finally, I broke down one day and called my dad and told him I thought I was "crazy" and that "something was not right with me." At the time, I was having issues with my friends because I was bottling up so many of my thoughts and feelings that I perceived were "wrong," which resulted in a meltdown. I didn't feel "right." I was feeling one thing, but behaving in another way in front of friends and family members. This meltdown happened at 21.

My dad was seeing a counselor at the time, so when I called him, he said he assured me and told me he would talk to his counselor and see if he knows someone who is an expert on anxiety. That didn't help and became a dead end.

One day I was driving back from college, and the radio was on. I heard an ad about a counseling service and immediately took their number. I got in touch with them, and they set me up with this amazing woman who changed my life for the better. I learned a great deal about my anxiety and its management. I learned and coped with it at my own pace, and my counselor helped me a great deal. The thing that helped me the most was knowing that I wasn't alone. We hear the slogan, "you are not alone," all the time, but believing it becomes a little hard when that is all you feel all the time. I thought I was a weird outcast, stuck in her twenties, wanting to have a normal life. But mere facts like maintaining eye contact with not only strangers but even your people was a tough job for me. I was labeled as shy and timid, but that is not what I felt. The simple act of just walking past people in the streets made me anxious because I just assumed everyone else had their life together, whereas I didn't. Going out with friends, interacting with a cashier, going to the gym, anything that involved people resulted in me questioning my self-worth.

Opening up about my experience changed my life entirely. When I was vulnerable, other people felt comfortable being vulnerable with me, and I realized everyone was struggling in their lives. Everyone had a similar story to tell or was going through something. It's okay to open up and share what you feel. You aren't alone, and everyone else is human at the end of the day".

- From a teenager

"Sitting at my desk in my science class, I found it very hard to concentrate. The dry topic and boring voice of my teacher made me think about everything else but what she was teaching. I was still upset about the morning. I hated myself because my parents never felt happy with me.

They nag at me for everything. Why didn't you clean your room? Why are you coming home late? B is just not enough; what am I going to do in my life? Jeez, give me a break! I am only 15 years old. I have more than enough time to figure my life out and learn every different skill set there has to be on earth. And as if that wasn't enough, my boyfriend broke up with me for another girl in school, and my best friend had ditched me for her new math nerd.

I am going to fail this math class, I thought to myself. And suddenly, my heart started beating fast. Cold sweats covered my forehead, and I started feeling dizzy. I tried to focus back on what my teacher was saying, thinking I might be able to distract my brain but to no avail. It started getting worse. I felt like he was speaking in slow motion. My chest started feeling heavy, and suddenly it felt like I was unable to breathe. Things started to become blurry, and I grasped at my desk, frantically.

This was the first time of the many time; a panic attack took over me. After that, through my classes and other life situations, I started losing myself to a heart beating faster than normal, cold sweats, and dizziness. It made me think that something was wrong with me, and that sowed the seed of self-doubt. I started questioning everything I did and thought.

My parents noticed this change in me and took me to the doctor. The doctor diagnosed me with an anxiety disorder and referred me to a counselor. At first, it was very hard for me to accept, let alone cope with this new condition. But now that I look back into time, I realized that I am glad I started seeing a counselor right away. It helped me in so many ways. My counselor made me realize I wasn't alone and helped me cope with my anxiety in a better manner. I heard stories about other people going through the same thing and connected with them. I think speaking about it makes things easier. It doesn't make you feel like you are the worst person on the planet. All those thoughts that throw you into self-doubt and make you question everything you do don't haunt you anymore. You don't FEEL alone. Because that's the worst feeling ever, to belittle yourself and to think that you don't have anyone else to share your fears with".

So WHY does talking about anxiety, depression, stress, and other mental health issues help?

It helps by giving you a chance to get those feelings and thoughts off of your chest. You discover that you are not alone and that many others experience similar issues. You get advice and tips to cope better with your situation. By talking, you get to know and can become a part of support networks. Support networks are all about giving and receiving support. It's about helping people. By talking, you break the stigma attached to mental health, and believe me! That helps a hundred others with you. By raising awareness and helping promote good mental health, you are saving lives.

CHAPTER 2: BREAKING IT DOWN

Defining a social situation

So what exactly is the social situation? A social situation is defined by the presence of at least one other person with you. Two main categories define a social situation: Performance situations and interactive exchange.

- Performance situations

    These are situations where people realize that they are being observed by someone else. Examples include: presenting at a meeting or in class, speaking in public, taking part in meetings or asking and answering questions in class, eating in front of other people, using public washrooms, writing something on the board, signing a check, filling out a form, performing in public such as singing or acting on stage or playing a sport and into a room full of people.

- Interactive exchange is a situation where people mingle with each other to form a closer relationship. Examples include: meeting new people, going out with co-workers or friends, inviting colleagues to do activities together, going to parties and dinners, going out on a date with someone, Putting your foot down to be assertive, saying out what is on your mind and expressing your opinion, having a conversation on the phone, working with co-workers on a project in a group, ordering food at a café, going to the store to return something and going for a job interview.

We aren't saying that generally people DON'T feel nervous in any social situation. It is not uncommon for people to be uneasy in some social situations and feel comfortable in others. For example, some people are relaxed while spending time with friends and family and interacting socially with co-workers they have worked with for a significant period but become extremely nervous about performing on stage or speaking in a business meeting. Some people are scared to be in a certain kind of situations such as public speaking or singing, while others generally avoid a larger number of social interactions.

Putting a face to social anxiety

To define what social anxiety looks like, here are a few things that describe how people with social anxiety feel when they are exposed to a social situation:

-People with social anxiety develop negative thoughts about themselves pretty quickly. For example: "I will forget what I have to say," "I will be speechless," "Other will think I am incompetent." They are also quick to assume that other people will think negatively about them.

- People who experience social anxiety also tend to focus their attention on themselves during social interaction. They are unable to stop thinking about their performance, their outlook, and how anxious they look and portray it to others. For example: "I will say something completely wrong or irrelevant," "People won't agree with me," "Everyone will dislike me," "I will offend someone."

- Individuals who experience social anxiety are often very worried about visible signs of anxiety, including blushing, shaking, or feeling sweaty. They are usually troubled by a racing heart, upset stomach, excessive sweating, blushing, having a choking sensation, dry mouth, trouble breathing, nausea, dizziness, blurred vision, and the urge to urinate repeatedly.

- To avoid the inconvenience of these symptoms and the "funny feeling," people with social anxiety often try to avoid social interactions. If they have to go one, they end up doing things that make them feel less anxious to keep them safe from embarrassment or negative judgment. For example: "I will avoid saying anything at all so that I don't end up saying anything stupid." They tend to avoid going to the event altogether, or even when they do; they leave early. They are often found engaging in protective behaviors to stay out of trouble. They would often be seen drinking alcohol, staying quiet, and avoiding eye contact.

What's happening in an anxious brain?

Anxiety itself is a natural human response that has a specific purpose. We should think about completely getting rid of it. The goal should be to culminate in our lives in a healthy and manageable way. Anxiety is part of our system, just like other emotions such as stress, sadness, dismay, and joy. The important point is to understand it and figure out a way to cope with it.

Simply defined, anxiety is a sense of fear and exaggerated nervousness that puts you on high alert. Scientifically, it is about an inflated sense of awareness to prepare us for a potential threat. Sadly, when we feel anxious excessively or are in a constant state of anxiety, we have a developed a problem for ourselves. Our bodies are stimulated by a constant fight or flight response, and we get affected by it physically as well as emotionally on the daily, even when no apparent reason or factors is triggering it.

Anxiety can mimic stress, but the real picture is much more complex than that. Anxiety can be caused by stress, but stress can present in other ways as well. Stressors can make an individual sad, angry, or worried, whereas anxiety especially makes a person feel fear, dread, and uneasiness. In some cases, it may not even be triggered by any specific reason, and you may just develop it on your own, whereas stress usually results from an external factor. Anxiety can be entirely due to an internal response. This is what makes anxiety essentially different from stress.

A few parts of the brain are pertinent to the generation of fear and anxiety. Using MRI and neurochemical techniques, scientists have discovered that the amygdala and the hippocampus play a huge role in multiple anxiety disorders.

The amygdala is an almond-shaped structure situated in the mid-brain and is believed to be the center of communication between various parts of the brain. It forms a connection between the parts of the brain that receive signals from the body and the parts that read and understand these signals to generate an appropriate response for the body. It is responsible for alerting the brain of imminent danger and triggering a fear or anxiety response. The memories related to emotions are also stored in the central part of the amygdala and may play a huge role in triggering anxiety and fear, such as fear of snakes, dogs, or spiders.

Another part of the brain – the hippocampus, processes, and stores hazardous events into memories. Hippocampus is implanted deep into each cerebral cortex's temporal lobe. This is an essential part of the limbic system, a cortical area where motivation, emotions, learning, and memory are regulated. Some studies have shown that the hippocampus is relatively smaller in people who were subjected to trauma during their childhood or were a part of the army. Hippocampus functions as an evaluation center that is responsible for behavioral restrictions, obsessional thinking, scanning, and spatial development.

The feeling of anxiety is part of your body's stress response. Your fight and flight response is in overdrive, and your systems are flushed with cortisol and norepinephrine. Both hormones are designed to give you a head start in perception, reflexes, speed, and dangerous situations. They increase your heart rate and allow extra blood to flow in your muscles, extra air to flow into your lungs, and overall prepare your body to counter a dangerous situation. Your body entirely focuses on developing survival traits, and it all shuts down once you are out of danger.

The way stress affects us is pretty well understood, but it is still in question of how exactly does anxiety operates? When and how does our body decide to anxious and what divides the area between feeling anxious and having anxiety affect us.

According to research, there many different psychological theories that explain how anxiety operates. The psychoanalytical theory explains anxiety as a fight between the id, ego, and superego. During this fight, anxiety provides that threat to a person's ego or superego, causing them to think that they are at an increased risk to act upon a small id instinct, and hence, a person's ego responds by trying to fix their id impulses by an exaggerated response.

Anxiety is a warning sign that you're about to do something you should or may not want to do. The cognitive theory describes that anxiety results when an individual's cognitive disruption or impractical thought process makes their body perceive everything as a threat, even if it doesn't pose any actual physical threat.

Another theory, called the behavioral theory, suggests that anxiety is an adaptive response due to excessive exposure to scary or traumatic circumstances.

Despite all these theories, it's extremely harmful to your body when these false instincts are repeatedly turned on to invoke a response. Your body's stress response is something designed to be engaged when needed and then turned off, whereas constant anxiety keeps us on a high alert and at an edge at all times.

Anxiety, whether triggered by genetics or raised in an anxiety-triggering environment including noisy places or parents and teacher who shout all the time, the issue occurs when the body and brain are "wired" to search for possible threats that may come from any direction, actual or perceived at any given time. Anything that could cause an unnecessary emotion to be it fear, anger, or doubt, or a trigger for anxiety – and if you establish thought patterns that reinforce every event in your life as a threat, it becomes an endless loop.

It's a challenge when you know that your anxiety doesn't seem to go anywhere, so you deal with it every day. For some people, this is harder than others. If you have been experiencing anxiety for a long period, it just becomes a part of you, and you might not even realize that it's a problem.

CHAPTER 3: WHAT IS YOUR THOUGHT PATTERN?

When does anxiety start to handicap you?

It is quite alright to feel anxious in certain situations. It is part of our normal response to certain situations. For example, quite a lot of people feel anxious before and during job interviews or while delivering formal speeches. It turns into a problem when social anxiety becomes too intense or starts happening in any and every social situation. When this starts to happen, it causes significant distress and affects many parts of a person's life.

When social anxiety turns into a full-blown problem, it starts to affect work and school life. People find it hard to sit in job interviews; they have problems interacting with their bosses or colleagues, they are extremely hesitant to ask questions and answers in during meetings or classes, they refuse job promotions, they avoid a specific kind of job or choose different career paths, they have poor performance at work and school, and they don't usually enjoy hours spent at work or in school.

They have trouble maintaining relationships. They don't have a lot of friends. They find it hard to keep friendships and maintain romantic relationships. They find it hard to open up to others and rarely share their problems.

People with social anxiety avoid trying new stuff. They try to miss out on classes and lessons from the fear of walking it a classroom full of students; they avoid activities that include interacting with other people, such as going to the gym or parties. They also find it hard to complete daily activities such as going to grocery shopping or eating out with family, taking the bus, or merely asking for directions. They specifically avoid social situations such as parties or intimate gatherings where they are not familiar with many people. They avoid interacting with authority figures or famous people. They don't particularly like being introduced to new people in settings where they are expected to talk. Some may even not like taking or making phone calls. They hesitate in asking for help or directions in stores, restaurants, from public servants, or people on the street. People suffering from anxiety avoid family reunions, especially where distant relatives make an appearance. They don't like or avoid standing in line at stores, banks, government offices with people who like to start a conversation in line. They avoid talking on internet forums and chatrooms where comments suggesting disapproval is expected.

These people harbor a constant fear of being negatively judged based on insufficient social interaction. They constantly worry about saying or doing embarrassing things. They feel excessively awkwardness or inferiority when they around important people. They hardly present their opinions or initiate a conversation. They don't do so because they think they will be perceived as stupid or annoying. People suffering from anxiety feel this immense satisfaction when they get praised or appreciated by others. They go out of their way to avoid being the center of attention. They often experience anticipatory anxiety where they start feeling nervous even before they become a part of a social situation.

It not limited to behavior. Social anxiety can have some pretty drastic effects on your body. Physical symptoms of social anxiety include derealization, feeling of unreality, feeling of detachment from oneself, palpitations, tachycardia, paresthesia, diarrhea, dizziness, and headaches. For specific individuals, these physical symptoms become so severe that it progresses to a panic attack. But in the case of people suffering from anxiety, they know that their panic attack is triggered by fear of interacting in social situations as compared to ones who have a panic disorder.

Social anxiety disorder manifests differently in adolescents and children. Younger children with anxiety may stick to their parent's side. They may become irritated and shout when brought into a social situation. They would routinely refuse to play with other kids, cry or complain about trouble with their stomach or other physical symptoms. Behavioral changes early on and fear of interacting in social situations early on may result in social anxiety later.

Anxiety also affects short-term memory. If you notice that you have forgotten events and things that happened during the period you were feeling anxious, it is quite common and happens with an anxiety disorder. This is due to increased cortisol from chronic anxiety that causes the hippocampus to shrink. Hippocampus is the memory center of the brain, as well. Constant anxiety leads to forgetfulness and confusion. This, however, specifically happens for chronic anxiety.

Anxiety can make you take rash decisions. It is mainly due to the effects of cortisol on the prefrontal cortex, which is mainly in charge of making decisions in our brain. It can lead to impulsive behavior and inappropriate decision making.

Anxiety and depression are very closely related. Anxiety can very often mimic the symptoms of depression. Many people suffer from depression as part of their anxiety disorder, and anxiety itself manifests as a symptom of depressive disorders. Both these conditions also share identical treatment options, including psychological counseling.

Anxiety is often described as a cause of insomnia. It is worse to get anxious at night and find it impossible to find sleep. It causes insomnia by activating the sympathetic nervous system similar to during the fight or flight response. This increases our heart rate, breathing, and brain waves, which causes wakefulness.

People with anxiety disorder develop a very sensitive amygdala. Amygdala is responsible for processing emotions and storing them. In this case, it overreacts to situations that aren't dangerous and triggers the brain circuit to react as if the body is an emergency. In the long term, anxiety becomes linked with these memories that trigger a feeling of danger and threat and generates its fears.

CHAPTER 4: WHEN AND WHERE DOES SOCIAL ANXIETY STRIKE

Social anxiety is not a condition but a disease, a disease that needs to be taken seriously by our society. It is a mental health condition in which the fear of being negatively evaluated by people makes one nervous and uncomfortable in a social situation. The stress of these situations weighs heavily on the patient, which makes it impossible for them to thrive in such a situation. Often people facing social anxiety avoid things people consider 'normal' such as small talk and eye contact because it makes them uncomfortable and sparks a feeling of unease so much so that their surroundings can turn into a virtual prison. Social anxiety disorder is common, and several people are diagnosed with it.

Different sceneries and situations are likely to evoke social fears. Learning about the sort of circumstances that could stimulate one's social anxiety disorder does not only help one cope with daily life hurdles but also make them aware of why their body is acting the way it is and signal to take precautionary measures. Now we will discuss some more common social anxiety triggers:

Often people with SAD find it difficult to carry out activities which are accompanied by an audience, for example, athletic races, public speaking, stage dramas, meetings, conferences, etc. they often feel judged and embarrassed, because they become insecure about the way other people will perceive hence resulting in their body reacting to it negatively for example in forms of excessive sweating, raced heartbeat, shivering, inability to maintain eye contact or to initiate conversation. People with SAD often find it difficult to carry out the small talk, and they fear that they might say something inappropriate, which may result in a negative image of them in front of others hence why small talk is extremely challenging for them, and often they avoid it. Things like dating can be stressful; for everybody, but people with SAD can be exhausting and traumatic if not dealt the right way. Let it be making love to your partner or calling them; all of it can create serious panic and trigger their anxiety. Often when it comes to reading in high school, a lot of students' chickens out, some of them are SAD patients and reading in front of a group can be a living nightmare for them, even writing while other people are watching the, can be stressful and lead to their handwriting being shaky. Sometimes to figure out if one has SAD, they must ask themselves some questions. Do you dislike expressing an opinion? Is agreeing with others the only option you opt for? If the answer is yes, Well, the chances are they may have SAD because often people who suffer from SAD would not express their views and input on certain things, due to fear of being criticized and mocked by others. While being watched while doing something counts as a major trigger for someone suffering from SAD, even basic things like eating food or drinking in front of people can be demanding and tough, as the idea of spilling your drink or dropping your food just keeps your mind occupied making one feeling pressurized. Ordering food from restaurants can also become nerve-racking for a SAD patient. Being bullied in high school or even at the workplace, being teased or picked at can make situations worse for someone suffering from SAD because it harshly triggers their anxiety-causing severe panic attacks as well, that's why always be considerate about the people in your surroundings. Reaching out to people in times of need, let it be from a coworker at work or shop keeper at the supermarket or a friend for advice can be troublesome for a person with SAD, that is another reason why we must offer help if we witness fellow beings having trouble in encountering a particular job. Large gatherings and parties are not the places for People with SAD, even lots of friends are not their cup of tea, often they are unable to express their grief to someone going through a tough time due to the fear of saying something wrong, but that doesn't mean that they don't care, it's just the situations which results in people with SAD opting a way of life which has the least social interactions. In a world of technology and advancement, A person with SAD is not likely to be active or interactive in terms of posting regularly about their lives on social media; they may even avoid group conversations because it can be a trigger to their anxiety for not being able to fit in the social media 'culture'.

It is a very serious condition, and hence somebody facing this disorder must reach out for medical help as not only will it help them strive better through daily struggles and interactions but also help them cope up with their anxiety better. Other than that, if someone has a social anxiety disorder, they can take the following precautions to make their stressful lives easier. First of all, You should do your extensive research about social anxiety disorder and be your own advocate so that you can make better life choices, always remember, reaching out for help from a colleague or a friend is normal and can be done without feeling embarrassed. If one is suffering from SAD, they must take up programs or raining to improve tier social interactive skills; many specially designed programs provide a platform for people suffering from a social anxiety disorder to cope up with such situations without triggering their anxiety. Starting a journal where you note down all your triggers and situations, which made you feel uneasy, can help you to cater to every circumstance individually. You can also consult a therapist who will help you decipher the underlying causes or events which stimulated this disorder; their expert advice will not only help you with social encounters but also tame down your anxiety. If you're facing panic attacks regularly, then taking medical help can help where your doctor may prescribe suitable medications. Research show practices like meditation and yoga help a lot in controlling anxiety, as it makes you in charge of your body and quiets the overactive brain, anxiety can be extremely overwhelming with all the thoughts and emotions weighing on your head, but meditation allows one to stopover attending to their emotions and thoughts and cultivates the approach of nonjudgmental acceptance when one becomes attentive to the present through meditation, it becomes easier for them to counter mental stress in social situations.

Try to give a chance to new opportunities, something you are passionate about so that the inner drive to do that thing can help you overcome your anxiety when dealing with other people. While you are at, don't forget to go easy on yourself; try celebrating yourself and your small everyday accomplishments. Managing and prioritizing things that provide you inner satisfaction can help reduce anxiety. Alcohol and drugs can only worsen anxiety and cause you to take unpredicted and fatal decisions, hence why stay clear of unhealthy substance use as it is not an escape but a permanent road to damage. Highly caffeinated tea or coffee is also not suggested to a SAD patient, because it can trigger the 'fight' or 'flight' response, it makes you overreact to situations which aren't dangerous or worrisome, increased caffeine can also make your anxiety worse after all taking precautionary measures only help you.

CHAPTER 5: ACTION PLAN

Social Anxiety Disorder can hinder the sufferer from reaching out for help. The fact that disorder disables the patient from striving through social interaction because of the fear of being judged makes them left with very little options when it comes to coping with their illness. Hence this a guide book on the next steps you should take if a social anxiety disorder is hindering your daily life activities.

Rule number one of dealing with SAD is being 'Aware.' When they said knowledge is power, they weren't wrong. Being educated about your symptoms and accepting that you may be going through mental illness is a step forward to becoming better. Research about your symptoms, and note down possible triggers, make a whole draft of how this disorder is affecting your life. Once you are fully educated on your condition, then you are ready for step two; Mindfulness. By focusing your entire attention on the very instant, one can counter rumination and worrisome. Thinking too much about the future or reminiscing can boost anxious feelings. Hence mindfulness helps you be aware of the current situation and allow more adaptive reactions. Trying out relaxation and correct breathing techniques has also led to positive outcomes in dealing with anxiety, as per research. Moreover, extensive cognitive and behavioral therapy aids in favorable consequences in terms of dealing with a social anxiety disorder. Following a healthy lifestyle by carrying out dietary adjustments can result in a stronger coping mechanism when it comes to SAD, for example, increasing the portion of magnesium in your diet, which is responsible for the tissues to relax hence reducing anxiety. Occasionally exercising can be helpful as exercise helps to bun stress chemicals and promotes relaxations; furthermore, physical exercise helps reduce and manage anxiety, so joining yoga groups can help with SAD at a great level. Being assertive and communicating your wants, needs, feelings in an honest way without intentionally offending someone can help you overcome your anxiety of being judged. Accepting yourself for who you are can help you thrive forward with this disorder faster; hence you can bypass problems like isolation and feelings of guilt more easily.

Reaching out to a doctor should be one of the first options to opt, as a medical expert will carry out an extensive diagnosis on several factors. For example:

1. The thought of meeting new people or being watched while you carry out daily activities such as eating or writing kindles anxiety and fear in you.

2. The intensity of your anxiety is double the actual threat of the circumstance.

3. You do not express your views or opinions on topics due to the fear of being criticized by people. You fear being rejected based on how you have symptoms of anxiety

4. The duration of your anxiety is above six months.

5. The fear of anxiety has led to hurdles in your essential aspects of life, including daily interactions and at the workplace.

6. The cause of these symptoms is not due to unhealthy substance use, such as drugs.

The following attached is a self-assessment questionnaire designed by the Anxiety and Depression Association of America to help to determine more about your condition if you are suffering from a set of given symptoms mentioned above.

This is a screening measure to help you determine whether you might have social anxiety that needs professional attention. This screening tool is not designed to make a diagnosis of social anxiety but to be shared with your primary care physician or mental health professional to inform further conversations about diagnosis and treatment.

Directions:

1. Print out the form

2. Complete the provided form

3. Share them with your health care provider to determine a diagnosis

Are you troubled by the following?

Intense and persistent fear of a social situation in which people might judge you, such as:

☐ Yes ☐ No

Social interactions (e.g., having a conversation, meeting unfamiliar people)

☐ Yes ☐ No

Being observed (e.g., eating or drinking in public)

☐ Yes ☐ No

Performing in front of others (e.g., giving a speech)

☐ Yes ☐ No

Fear that you will act in a way or show anxiety symptoms that will be negatively evaluated (i.e., will be humiliating or embarrassing; will lead to rejection or offend others)

☐ Yes ☐ No

Fear that people will notice that you are blushing, sweating, trembling, or showing other signs of anxiety

☐ Yes ☐ No

Perceiving that your reaction to feared situations to be greater than most other people

☐ Yes ☐ No

Doesafeared situation cause you to...?

☐Yes☐ No

Alwaysfeelanxious?

☐ Yes ☐ No

Experience a panic attack, during which you suddenly is overcome by intense fear or discomfort, including any of these symptoms:

☐ Yes ☐ No

Pounding heart

☐ Yes ☐ No

Sweating

☐ Yes ☐ No

Trembling or shaking

☐ Yes ☐ No

Choking

☐ Yes ☐ No

Chest pain

☐ Yes ☐ No

Trembling or shaking

☐ Yes ☐ No

Nausea or abdominal discomfort

☐ Yes ☐ No

"Jelly" legs

☐ Yes ☐ No

Dizziness

☐ Yes ☐ No

Feelings of unreality or being detached from yourself

☐ Yes ☐ No

Fear of losing control or "going crazy."

☐ Yes ☐ No

Fear of dying

☐ Yes ☐ No

Numbness or tingling sensations

☐ Yes ☐ No

Chills or hot flushes

☐ Yes ☐ No

Go to great lengths to avoid participating?

☐ Yes ☐ No

Have your symptoms interfered with your daily life?

Having more than one illness at the same time can make it difficult to diagnose and treat different conditions. Depression and substance abuse are among the conditions that occasionally complicate social anxiety disorder.

☐ Yes ☐ No

Have you experienced changes in sleeping or eating habits?

More days than not, do you feel...

☐ Yes ☐ No

Sad or depressed?

☐ Yes ☐ No

Disinterested in life?

☐ Yes ☐ No

Worthless or guilty?

During the last year, it has the use of alcohol or drugs...

☐ Yes ☐ No

Resulted in your failure to fulfill responsibilities with work, school, or family?

☐ Yes ☐ No

Placed you in a dangerous situation, such as driving a car under the influence?

☐ Yes ☐ No

Gottenyouarrested?

☐ Yes ☐ No

Continueddespitecausingproblems for you or your loved ones?

☐ Yes ☐ No

Reference: Diagnostic and Statistical Manual of Mental Disorders, Fourth Edition. Washington, DC, American Psychiatric Association, 1994.

During the last year, it has the use of alcohol or drugs...

During the past six months, have you often been bothered by any of the following symptoms? Check one square next to each symptom that you have had more days than not:

	Not at all	A little	Moderately	Quite a bit	Extremely
a. restlessness or feeling keyed up or on edge	⓪	① ②	③ ④	⑤ ⑥	⑦ ⑧
b. Irritability	⓪	① ②	③ ④	⑤ ⑥	⑦ ⑧
c. difficulty falling/staying asleep or restless/unsatisfying sleep	⓪	① ②	③ ④	⑤ ⑥	⑦ ⑧
d. being easily fatigued	⓪	① ②	③ ④	⑤ ⑥	⑦ ⑧
e. difficulty concentrating or mind going blank	⓪	① ②	③ ④	⑤ ⑥	⑦ ⑧

f.　　　muscle　⓪　①②　③④　⑤⑥　⑦⑧
tension

How much do worry and physical symptoms interfere with your life, work, social activities, family, etc.?

⓪　　　①②　　③④　　　⑤⑥　　　⑦⑧
None　　Mild　　Moderate　　Severe　　V e r y
　　　　　　　　　　　　　　　　　　Severe

How much are you bothered by worry and physical symptoms (how much distress does it cause you)?

⓪　　　①②　　③④　　　⑤⑥　　　⑦⑧
None　　Mild　　Moderate　　Severe　　V e r y
　　　　　　　　　　　　　　　　　　Severe

Source: Newman, M. G., Zuellig, A. R., Kachin, K. E., Constantino, M. J., Przeworski, A., Erickson, T., &Cashman-McGrath, L. (2002). Preliminary reliability and validity of the GeneralizedAnxietyDisorder Questionnaire-IV: A revised self-report diagnostic measure of generalized anxiety disorder. BehaviorTherapy, 33, 215-233. doi:10.1016/S0005-7894(02)80026-0.

CHAPTER 6: SAYING BYE TO YOUR FEARS AND HELLO TO A NEW LIFE

Treatment decisions are based on how your anxiety affects you and what role it plays in your daily life. The mainstay of treatment for generalized anxiety disorders is psychotherapy and medications. It depends on how each affects you based on the kind of symptoms you have. You may benefit from both the therapies combined, or it may take some time for you to adjust to either one of them.

Psychotherapy

Psychotherapy, also known as talk therapy or psychological treatment, requires working with a therapist to reduce anxiety symptoms. The most common method of psychotherapy for generalized anxiety disorder is cognitive-behavioral therapy.

Cognitive-behavioral therapy (CBT) is typically a short-term procedure that focuses on teaching you practical strategies to handle your problems directly and help you slowly adjust to the behavior you have avoided because of anxiety. During this phase, as you build upon your initial progress, your symptoms improve.

CBT is the most widely used treatment for people who have social phobia. It recognizes the way a person thinks (cognition) and behaves (behavior) influences their feelings. A practitioner who uses CBT to help a person with a social phobia should typically provide cognitive therapy, graded exposure, and training in social skills.

CBT's cognitive therapy aspect aims to help people with social phobia analyze problem forms of thinking and question certain patterns of thinking. This involves focusing on the underlying and troubling feelings about oneself and others. Because people with social phobia tend to avoid stressful environments, graded exposure is a vital aspect of CBT. Therapists help people become more relaxed in the situation, which causes anxiety in them.

CBT can be performed either individually or in a group session. For treating social phobia, group therapy is also recommended.

Psychotherapy is an important aspect of psychiatric therapy. It applies to learn about the anxiety signs and why they arise. For example, if people are aware of the human physiological reaction to fear, they appear to be less fearful of symptoms. People respond to the threat of imminent danger with an acute reaction to fight or flight, during which several physiological changes occur. These changes include the release of hormones from the brain, including adrenaline, muscle tension, and increased breathing rate.

Knowing the anxiety symptoms and why they occur can help the person become less anxious about the symptoms themselves.

Comprehension of this cycle will also help the individuals understand the value of breathing, relaxation, and aerobics exercise. Breathing and calming techniques are often taught to reduce physical anxiety effects and control stress in a better manner.

Medication

Many forms of drugs, including those below, are used to treat generalized anxiety disorder. Review the advantages of risks and potential side effects with your doctor.

Antidepressants, including the selective serotonin reuptake inhibitor (SSRI) and serotonin and norepinephrine reuptake inhibitors (SNRI), are used the first-line therapies. Types of antidepressants pertinent in the treatment of generalized anxiety disorders include escitalopram, duloxetine, venlafaxine, and paroxetine. Other antidepressants can also be prescribed by the doctor.

Buspirone – the antianxiety drug called Buspirone is used regularly and, like many other anxiolytics, takes several weeks to show its effects.

Benzodiazepine - Benzos, often referred to as sedatives, are intended for use only over a brief period (two-three weeks) or when used intermittently as part of a comprehensive treatment program and not as the primary or sole treatment.

A person receiving care for social anxiety follows a different path of recovery as compared to some other person who suffers from a similar condition. Recovery will include ups and downs, with some days being better than others.

- Speak to your doctor about a referral to a mental health provider who is specialized in social phobia care.

- Note the patterns of thought which contribute to your anxiety. Write down these and see if you can contest them on your own. Then talk to a health professional you trust to discuss them.
- Set practical and easily achievable goals. Walk three days a week, for example, take a yoga class and eat daily meals.

- Note the spread of avoidance: It seems like when a person begins avoiding one case, it is more likely that they will avoid others. Instead, tr approaching situations step by step. Face the worries. Set concrete targets that reflect the tasks you want to achieve.

- Learn and practice strategies for controlling anxiety, such as respiratory and relaxation techniques. Breathing and calming strategies can help alleviate anxiety and stress overall if practiced regularly.

- Repair the outline, a lot of time to work, but also relax. Do things that you enjoy and spend time with family and friends.
- Keep a healthy lifestyle. Get regular exercise to reduce anxiety, have adequate sleep, eat a balanced diet, and limit your intake of alcohol and other stimulants, such as caffeine.

Family and friends can play a significant role in helping a person recover from social phobia. There are also ways you can help yourself cope with caring for a socially phobic person. The more you know about this disease, the more you'll be of support.

Understand that the patient has an anxiety disorder and is not just a complicated one; anxiety is a very real and distressing experience.

Encourage the person to seek medical help by letting him/her know what resources are available and by promising to accompany the person when he/she visits the health care provider.

Don't get interested in avoiding the person's items or circumstances that make him/her nervous. Instead, empower the individual to deal step by step with their fears. When possible, provide practical support, such as being with an individual when faced with their anxiety – if the person is okay with you staying around.

Encourage the person to challenge unreasonable or nervous thoughts. Acknowledge any achievements, no matter how insignificant.

Work with individuals to restore an everyday routine that includes fun and calming activities.

Enable the adult to maintain a healthy lifestyle and participate in social activities.

Don't expect too much too soon. It can take some time to heal, and there may be ups and downs.

Find emotional help for yourself – sometimes, it can be difficult to communicate with and care about a person with social phobia.

You might need some help too. This may include joining a support group, counseling for people, couples or families, or educational sessions.

By now, are you wondering where to find help?

A general practitioner is a suitable person to address your issues initially. A good GP makes the diagnosis accurately, tests for any physical health conditions or medications that may lead to anxiety. Discusses available therapies and works with individuals to draw up a mental health treatment plan to allow a person suffering from anxiety to receive appropriate care. The GP provides treatment discounts and brief advice. In some cases, he also initiates talk therapy and prescribes medication.

It is recommended that people visit their usual GP or another GP at the same clinic because there is an exchange of medical knowledge within a clinic.
Psychologists are professionals who offer psychological treatments such as cognitive-behavioral therapy and interpersonal therapy. Registered psychologists specialize in mental health problems assessment, diagnosis, and treatment. Clinical psychologists are not physicians.

Psychiatrists, however, are physicians specialized in mental health. They receive specialized training in mental health. They are capable of doing medical and psychological examinations, do diagnostic testing, offer to counsel and prescribe medications. Psychiatrists often use therapies such as CBT and interpersonal therapy in combination with anxiolytics drugs. If the anxiety is serious and admission to the hospital is necessary, a doctor may be responsible for the care of the person.

The cost of getting treated by a health professional differs. However, there are opportunities where people get consultation fees subsidized when they see a mental health professional for the treatment of anxiety and depression.

CHAPTER 7: REWIRE YOUR ANXIOUS BRAIN

Aside from medicine, there are other methods you may use to help reduce symptoms of anxiety, from meditation to deep breathing exercises.

Furthermore, certain foods that you can consume can also help lower the severity of your symptoms, mainly because of their brain-boosting features.

Here we discuss a few essential foods and beverages that have proven to alleviate anxiety symptoms.

Salmon

Salmon may be helpful for anxiety reduction. It contains nutrients that support brain health, including eicosapentaenoic acid (EPA), vitamin-D and omega- 3 fatty acids and docosahexaenoic acid (DHA).

EPA and DHA can help control the dopamine and serotonin neurotransmitters, which can have a calming and relaxing effect.

Also, studies show that these fatty acids can reduce inflammation and prevent brain cell dysfunction, which leads to mental disorders such as anxiety. Consuming sufficient quantities of EPA and DHA will also enhance the capacity of your brain to adjust to changes, allowing you to manage stressors that helps alleviate the anxiety symptoms.

Vit D has also been investigated for the beneficial impact it may have on reducing neurotransmitter levels. Just a few servings of salmon in a week can serve to promote relief from anxiety.

According to research, people who consumed Atlantic salmon for five months, three times a week, showed less anxiety than those who consumed chicken, pork, or beef. They also had anxiety-related symptoms, such as heart rate and palpitations.

Chamomile

Chamomile is an herb that has the ability to help relieve anxiety. This contains high levels of antioxidants that have been shown to minimize inflammation, which in turn minimizes the risk of anxiety. The relationship between chamomile and relief from anxiety has been investigated in several studies. We found that those diagnosed with a widespread anxiety disorder reported substantially greater symptom reduction after eating chamomile extract relative to those who did not. The study showed similar findings as those who had eight weeks of drinking chamomile extract had decreased symptoms of depression and anxiety.

Although these findings are positive, the majority of studied on chamomile extract were performed to evaluate the anti-anxiety effects of chamomile tea, which is mostly consumed and works.

Magnesium

Magnesium is another element that may stave off nervous symptoms. Magnesium is a soothing mineral used to evoke relaxation, and a diet deficient in magnesium was found to aggravate anxiety symptoms. Research has shown that magnesium can also help cure other mental health problems. According to another research, insufficient magnesium decreases neurotransmitter serotonin rates, and it has been shown that antidepressants work by improving magnesium levels in the brain, which shows there is a positive connection. Magnesium functions on the blood-brain barrier to prevent stress hormones from reaching the brain.

Dark chocolate

The addition of some dark chocolate into your diet will also help to relieve anxiety. Dark chocolate contains flavonols, antioxidants that can be food for the brain function. They do so by enhancing blood flow to the brain and encouraging its adaptability to stressful conditions. Such effects allow you to better adapt to stressful conditions, which can lead to anxiety and other mood disorders. Some researchers also believe that the importance of dark chocolate in brain health may be simply due to its taste, which can be beneficial for those with mood disorders.

In a study, an individual who ate 74 percent dark chocolate twice daily for two weeks had decreased levels of stress hormones typically associated with anxiety. These hormones include epinephrine and cortisol. It has also been shown that eating dark chocolate raises the neurotransmitter serotonin levels, which may help to alleviate the tension that contributes to anxiety. For instance, participants reported significantly lower stress rates in a study of a highly stressed individual after eating 40 grams of dark chocolate per day over two weeks. Nevertheless, dark chocolate is best consumed in moderation because it is rich in calories and easy to overeat. The serving size of 1- 1.5 ounces is appropriate.

Yogurt

When you have anxiety, yogurt is a wonderful food that should be included in your diet. The probiotics or healthy bacteria found in some types of yogurt can help improve many parts of your health, including your mental health.

Studies have shown that probiotic foods such as yogurt can improve mental health and brain function by inhibiting free radicals and neurotoxins, which can damage the brain's nerve tissue and cause anxiety.

In a study, anxious individuals who daily consumed probiotics yogurt were able to cope with stress better than those who consumed yogurt without probiotics. Another research showed that women who ingested 44 ounces of yogurt twice daily for four weeks had greater functioning of the brain regions regulating emotions and sensation, which could be correlated with lower rates on anxiety.

Such results are positive, but there is a need for further human research to validate the beneficial impact that yogurt can have on reducing anxiety.

Green Tea

Green tea contains L-theanine, an amino acid studied for its beneficial effects on brain function and reduction of anxiety. In one small sample, people who ingested L-theanine experienced a decrease in responses to psychological stress that are usually associated with anxiety, such as elevated heart rate. Another research showed that those who drank a beverage containing L-theanine had reduced levels of cortisol, an anxiety-linked stress hormone. Such findings may be attributed to the ability of L-theanine to avoid overexcitation of the nerves. Also, L-theanine can increase neurotransmitters with anti-anxiety effects.

Additionally, green tea contains epigallocatechin gallate (EGCG), an antioxidant that is recommended for brain safety. While also through GABA in the brain (42Trusted Source), it may play a role in reducing other symptoms. One mouse research showed that EGCG developed similar anti-anxiety effects on traditional anxiety medicines. L-theanine and EGCG's beneficial properties could be a major reason why drinking many cups of green tea every day is correlated with less psychological distress.

Although all of these results are positive, it is worth noting that most works on green tea and anxiety were conducted in animals and test tubes. The further human study is required to validate its effects on anti-anxiety. Other Foods that may help with anxiety, although some of the foods listed below, have not been explicitly tested for their effects on anti-anxiety; they are rich in nutrients that are thought to improve associated symptoms.

Turkey, bananas, and oats: These are good sources of the amino acid tryptophan, which is converted to serotonin in the body and may promote relaxation and anxiety relief. Eggs, meat, and dairy products: All provide high-quality protein, including essential amino acids that produce the neurotransmitters dopamine and serotonin, which have the potential to improve mental health.

Chia seeds: Chia seeds are another strong source of brain-boosting omega-3 fatty acids that have been shown to help in anxiety.

Citrus fruits and bell peppers: These fruits are rich in vitamin C, which has antioxidant properties that may help reduce inflammation and prevent damage to cells that may promote anxiety.

Almonds: Almonds provide a significant amount of vitamin E, which has been studied for its role in anxiety prevention.

Blueberries: Blueberries are high in vitamin C and other antioxidants, such as flavonoids, that have been studied for their ability to improve brain health and thus help with anxiety relief.

Physicians also know how to relieve or cure anxiety with medication and medications, but the key to soothing the disorder may be plain sight hiding: the foods we consume. Doctors and nutritionists are starting to learn more about how some or lack of nutrients affect the brain. "Our brain has very high demands on resources and nutrients," says

Melissa Reagan Brunetti, CNC, a clinical nutritionist, and wellness coach. Nutritional deficiencies and dietary habits may impair their function, and change brain chemistry and neurotransmitter formulations— chemicals in the brain that can stimulate and calm down. Research by Ohio State University showed that one nutrient that is especially effective at reducing nervous symptoms is omega-3 fatty acids, found in fatty fish such as wild salmon, flaxseed, walnuts, and chia seeds. To function properly, our brains need fat from dietary sources. If you don't eat enough healthy fats, the brain will suffer.

Harvard Medical School recommends eating foods that are high in B vitamins, such as beef, avocado, and almonds, to help protect against nervous feelings. B vitamins have positive effects on the nervous system, and deficiencies were associated with anxiety disorders. Vitamin B6 is helping the body make several neurotransmitters, including serotonin, that influence mood, according to the University of Maryland Medical Center. Research from Australia showed that after 12 weeks, stressed-out staff delivering a high dose of B vitamins felt less depressed and in a better mood. Another study, from the University of Miami, showed that, after two months, depressed adults taking a vitamin B complex had less depressive and anxious symptoms. Another nutrient that seems to matter is choline found in eggs, a cousin of B vitamins. More work is needed, but promising are those findings.

We typically think of tryptophan as the ingredient in turkey that puts us to sleep after Thanksgiving — and in fact, tryptophan is an amino acid that the body uses to manufacture the serotonin neurotransmitter that helps to control sleep and moods. Tryptophan could help alleviate nervous feelings, according to the University of Michigan. In one small sample, participants who ate a tryptophan-bar registered fewer symptoms than those who ate a tryptophan-bar. Further work is required, but a link seems likely to exist. Tryptophan is present in most foods high in proteins, such as turkey and other meats, nuts, seeds, beans, and eggs. (Incidentally, protein is also essential for the development of dopamine on the neurotransmitter, which can also support mood.) These are the seven silent signs of high functioning anxiety.

While some of us feel unhappy before we have our cup of java in the morning, coffee, and other caffeinated foods and beverages simply exacerbate anxious feelings. It increases heart rate, blood pressure, and body temperature as it is a stimulant to the nervous system. Coffee can lead to troubling symptoms, such as nervousness, sweating, and trembling, according to the University of Michigan. Brazilian researchers found that caffeine did cause panic attacks in people with an anxiety condition. Another research by the University of Wake Forest found that caffeine decreased blood flow to the brain by 27 percent. Not to mention that sleep can mess, which is important for brain health. Limiting the consumption of caffeine will help to defeat the inflammation and help enhance brain function. Likewise, doctors recommend avoiding caffeinated energy drinks and indulging in too much dark chocolate (stick to one or two squares a day).

BERRY GREEN SMOOTHIE

Ingredients

- 2 cups loosely packed baby spinach

- 1 cup of unsweetened almond milk

- 1/2 cup of frozen blueberries

- 1/4 cup of frozen raspberries

- Two scoops Essential Proteins Collagen Peptides

- 1 tablespoon of nut butter

- 1 tablespoon of hemp or chia seeds

- 1/4-teaspoon of ground cinnamon

Instructions:

Place all the ingredients into a mixer.

Mix until smooth.

Notes

You can use any protein powder you want, but be mindful that flavored powders change the taste significantly.

BANANA - BERRY BAKED OATMEAL BITES

Ingredients

- 1 ripe banana

- 1 cup of almond milk

- 1 big egg

- 1/3 cup of pure maple syrup

- 1½ teaspoons of pure vanilla extract

- 1 teaspoon of coconut oil (in liquid form)

- 1 teaspoon of lemon zest

- 2 teaspoons of lemon juice

- 2 cups of gluten-rolled oats

- 1 teaspoon of cinnamon ground

- ½ teaspoon of kosher salt

- 1 tablespoon of cooking powder

- 1 cup of fresh blueberries (or berries of your choice)

Preheat the oven to 350 ° C.

Instructions

Spray cooking spray on a small muffin pot.

Place the banana in a big bowl and mash well with a fork. Add the almond milk, sugar, maple syrup, vanilla extract, coconut oil, lemon zest and juice, and whisk until well and smooth. Blend the oats, cinnamon, salt, and baking powder in a separate dish. Add dry ingredient to wet ingredients and mix with a whisk. Blueberries blend in.

In a prepared mini muffin pan, spoon the oatmeal mixture. The wells are nearly filled to the rim. You will have enough for 20 bites of oatmeal.

Bake for 18-minutes until the oatmeal has set, and slightly brown the tops of the pieces.

Let the morsels cool for 10 minutes in a muffin pan. Serve warm or move them carefully to a wire rack to cool completely and then cool/freeze in an airtight jar until you are ready to eat.

YOGA

It is estimated that Yoga originated in India more than 5,000 years ago. Derived from the ancient Sanskrit Indian language, the word yoga means "yoke" or "unite." Yoga practice involves body, mind, and spirit joining together. Yoga can help regain a sense of personal equilibrium through breathing exercises, meditation, gestures, and relaxation, and is another type of therapy that has been shown to help with an anxiety disorder.

Meditation and other stress-reduction methods have been studied since the 1970s as potential therapies for depression and anxiety, and yoga has gained less consideration to the medical literature, though in recent decades it has become increasingly popular. For example, one national survey reported that about 7.5 percent of U.S. adults had attempted yoga at least once and that almost 4 percent had done yoga in the previous year.

Yoga classes can vary from gentle and welcoming to strenuous and challenging; style choices tend to be based on physical ability and personal inclination. Hatha yoga, the most commonly performed form of yoga, incorporates three features: physical poses, called asanas; guided breathing in combination with asanas; and a brief duration of deep relaxation or meditation.

A wide variety of yoga activities available reports say they may reduce the effect of excessive stress responses and can be useful for both anxiety and depression. Yoga works in this way, like other self-relieving methods, such as meditation, recreation, exercise, or even mingling with friends.

Yoga tends to modulate stress response processes by raising perceived stress and anxiety. It, in effect, reduces physiological excitement — for example, reduced heart rate, lowering blood pressure, and easing breathing. There is also evidence that yoga practices are helping to improve variation in heart rate, a measure of the body's ability to respond more flexibly to stress.

While many types of yoga practice are healthy, some are strenuous and maybe not appropriate for everyone. For particular, older patients or those with movement problems may want to consult with a clinician first before selecting yoga as an option for treatment.

Yet yoga can be a very promising way to help control symptoms for many people who are struggling with depression, anxiety, or stress. Yes, the yoga science study indicates that mental and physical health are not only closely related but are practically identical. The proof that yoga practice is a fairly low-risk, high-yield method for improving overall health is growing. Yoga can also be a perfect way to get to know other people and to feel more connected to society. Certain individuals with anxiety and agoraphobia face issues of isolation and loneliness. Participating in a yoga class can be one way to start socializing when working for personal well-being.

Yoga postures for anxiety

The following series of yoga will help bring about a relaxed and balanced mind and body. Asanas help relieve tension and stress from the body by balancing hormones and elevating endorphins (which explains the "yoga high") in addition to many other benefits.

- Gentle Neck Rolling (KanthaSanchalana)• Cat Stretch (Marjariasana) • Baby Pose (Shishuasana) • Downward Facing Dog (AdhomukhaShwanasana) • Standing Forward Bend (Hastapadasana) • Tree Pose (Vrikshasana) • One-Legged Sitting Forward Bend (JanuSirsasana) • Two-Legged Sitting Forward Bend (Paschimottanasana)• Bridge Pose (Setubandhasana) • Shoulder stand (Sarvangasana) • Fish Pose (Sarvangasana) This technique is effective for flushing out body contaminants from the environment, a key source of stress.

Relaxation techniques to alleviate anxiety

Breathing exercises are an incredibly effective technique that can clear the mind and reduce stress within seconds. • Deep yogic breath • Alternative nostril breathing (Nadishodhan pranayama)• Victory breath (Ujjayi breathing) • Bellows breathing (Bhastrika pranayama)• Bee breath (Bhramaripranayama) 3. Bee breath (Bhramari pranayama)• Bee breath (Bhramari pranayama)

Exercise

Ever heard of the phrase "finding your happy place?" Creating a mental picture of a place where you feel relaxed will calm your brain and body. Sit in a quiet and relaxing place when you start to feel anxious. Think of your dream place to unwind. Although it can be anywhere in the world, whether actual or imaginary, it should be a picture you can find very relaxing, happy, peaceful, and secure. Make sure it's easy enough to think about, so when you feel nervous in the future, you can return to it in your mind. Talk about all the small things you would discover if you were there. Talk of the smell, look and sound that the place will have. Imagine being in that position, enjoying it peacefully. When you get a clear picture of your "happy spot," close your eyes and take long and frequent breaths out of your mouth and through your nose. Be mindful of your breathing and keep concentrating on the spot in your mind you've pictured until you feel your fear rising. If you feel nervous, visit this place in your mind.

You may find pain or stress in your muscles if you feel nervous. This muscle tension will make your anxiety easier to deal with at the moment you feel it. You will usually minimize your anxiety levels by relieving the tension in your muscles.

During periods of anxiety to quickly alleviate your muscle tension: sit in a quiet and relaxed position. Close your eyes and focus on breathing. Slowly breathe into your nose and out your mouth. You are using your hand to make your fist rigid. Squeeze firmly into your palm. Keep a few seconds with your hand clenched. Note all the stress in your hand that you experience. Open your fingers slowly, and be mindful of your thoughts. You may feel a feeling of tension leaving your side. Your hand will finally feel lighter and more relaxed. Keep tensing and then release specific muscle groups from your hands, legs, shoulders, or feet into your body. You may want to work your way up and down, tensing various groups of muscles. Avoid tensing the muscles in every part of your body where you're injured or in pain, because this can worsen the injury further.

Counting is a simple way to relieve the fear. Find a quiet and relaxing place to relax when you sense anxiety rushing over you. Close your eyes, and count to 10 slowly. Repeat and count to 20, or even higher, if appropriate. Keep counting until you feel the fear subsiding. Relief often comes fast, but other times it can take some time. Keep cool and stay vigilant. Counting will calm you because, besides your fear, it gives you something to concentrate on. It's a perfect resource to use in a crowded or busy space where other anxiety exercises may be more difficult to execute.

Mindfulness is the practice of being mindful without critical thinking, in your current state and environment. Staying present will help you maintain a relaxed state of mind when you feel running and build-up of fear in your mind. To get yourself into the moment outside of your thoughts: Find a quiet and relaxing place to sit and close your eyes. Remember how the body and breathing feel. Now transfer your focus to the sensations you see around you. Ask yourself: What's going on outside my body? Note what you are seeing, smelling, and sensing around you. Switch your focus from your body to your surroundings several times, and then back until your fear starts to fade.

We live in an age of terror. There are stressors around everywhere, with the relentless hustle and big and small worries. According to the American Anxiety and Depression Foundation, about 40 million U.S. adults currently live with an anxiety disorder. It can be daunting, to say the least, to speak from personal experience, in the age of constant streaming of knowledge, and a culture that encourages an attitude of keeping up with new advancements. After all, we are just human. There are only too many hours in the day. But no matter how many times we say these mantras, it's not enough to hold fear at bay, sometimes. That doesn't mean that you have to take a beach holiday or spend money at the spa. Instead, check out those inexpensive, usable products built specifically to cope with stress and worry. His connection to sleep is one of the most disturbing aspects of anxiety.

A 2018 study found that people with anxiety usually have poor sleep quality, and in effect, poor sleep quality can increase anxiety. If anxiety affects your sleep, negatively, you might want to consider using a weighted blanket. Weighted covers are medical covers, usually weighing between 5 and 30 pounds. They can help to ease pain, reduce anxiety, and boost mood.

If you choose to sleep hot or cold, pick one that is around 10 percent of your body weight, and look for features such as temperature-regulating properties. Stimulation of the deep pressure uses hand-on pressure to calm the nervous system. Doing so will help: alleviate pain-relieving anxiety, enhancing mood. Deep pressure relaxation doesn't have to be hands-on absolutely. The same pressure comes from getting the blanket wrapped around the body, with weighted blankets. Deep pressure stimulation has proved to be an important part of therapy.

Most aromatherapy studies indicate that essential oils can help to reduce anxiety. You may use essential oils in a variety of ways to create a warm, stress-free atmosphere, such as diffusing them into the air or applying them to your body. Notice that the Food and Drug Administration isn't restricting essential oils. And please make sure to buy from a reputable business while shopping for refill oils. Search for products that use pure and natural ingredients at 100 percent. There are plenty of knock-offs, like perfume oils that aren't as sweet.

Acupressure is a type of traditional Chinese medicine that works by boosting body pressure points. Research from 2015 found that while there is contradictory evidence about its effect on physiological anxiety indices, it is successful in providing overall anxiety relief. The most comprehensive way to practice is possible to see an acupressurist, but this is not always the preferable choice. An acupressure pad is an inexpensive and successful way to go if you want to try it yourself.

A good piece of news! Coloring doesn't just relate to girls. Coloring can help to decrease anxiety in adults. Several studies link coloring to attention and holding you at the moment. And if you feel nervous, consider sitting down with a fresh crayon box— who doesn't love a brand-new crayon box? — Now they have it. It's the coloring activity itself that's believed to center you, so it doesn't matter which book you want to draw. Yet this coloring book for adults has plenty of intricate designs and lovely patterns. Several users find the pages a little thin, so if you prefer using markers, it may not be the best option.

If your mind is in a million different places, it can be good when and where you can simplify a few little items. A purse organizer is an easy, budget-friendly way to free up a little brain space if you wear a purse and make sure you always know where it is. Rummaging for my keys or credit cards in less time saves precious seconds and tons of immediate tension.

Facial Gel Bead Eye Mask is an economical option, although a soothing facial may not always be in the budget. Pop it into the microwave and use it to relax before bedtime, or even during the day while taking a breather. The mask can also be frozen and used to help relieve pressure on the sinus, back pain, and headaches. Personal tip: Freezing a washcloth and pressing it over your eyes will do this on an even tighter budget.

To those who want to feel comfortable and alleviate stress, pain, and anxiety, shiatsu massage is the safest form of massage. It is a Japanese massage style which can help alleviate anxiety and depression. But in this day and age of stretching too thin, micromanaging schedules and living paycheck to paycheck, if you don't have time or resources to stop for a weekly massage, it's fully understandable. A portable massager is a cost-effective and reliable solution. Massagers of shiatsu come in all sizes and at all price points. There are Sun, Vibration, Different Intensities, and more choices. If you're not sure what's right for you, visiting a doctor or chiropractor might be a good idea to find out which alternative will better suit your needs.

A 2009 study found that in those with anxiety disorder, a sun lamp— which imitates natural outdoor light— can help improve mood and decrease depression and anxiety. When you spend a lot of time indoors and can't always get outside, it can also help year-round. Make sure to talk to your doctor before buying a sun lamp. Search for one with a 10,000 lux power, and be sure not to search straight at the sun. Try to do it every day at the same time.

CONCLUSION

Turn to relaxation methods: music, meditation, exercise, personal routines learning some good techniques of relaxation would be of benefit to you. Fast, accelerated respiration, for example, can sound too simple, but it's a great way to ease the body into a more comfortable state. It's something you can do before or after an occurrence at your work desk, in your car, and afterward. Breathe in for four seconds, then six seconds out. Count in your ear, and concentrate on your count and your breathing sensation. Repeat for as long as you need a little to relax.

Many studies promote visualization as a method of relaxation. Imagine living in the most comfortable environment you could think of, whether it's in bed at home or in the tropics on the beach. Wherever you think you'd be most comfortable, just pause and position yourself there mentally. When you're at the pool, ask yourself how warm it's and if the sky has clouds. Are you solitary? Is this real, or can you hear the ocean? The objective here is not only to create a perfect, calming picture in your head but also to get your brain to focus on those details— the more you do, the further away your mind will be from something that has caused your anxiety.

Art, exercise, or meditation may provide a similar impact. Relaxing music can help alleviate your fear from your mind or help you refocus after an anxious period. Exercise is similar, but it does have a psychological (as well as a physiological) effect, rather than just taking the mind away. The endorphins released during exercise in our brains make us happier, and the sense of accomplishment that we get from the regular activity will help to alleviate anxiety.

Meditation — especially directed meditation — can also help, because it's all about relaxing the mind and discarding the errant thoughts that lead to anxiety and stress. Meditation will help you concentrate on your surroundings or be mindful of the present, rather than allowing the past to be seen in the foreground.

Finally, turn to your habits of relaxation to take the edge off your anxiety. If you have none, make new ones. These can do wonders for your mental and emotional health, and make sure you have good behaviors and routines that you can turn to when you're depressed or nervous, so negative behaviors don't take root.

We've spoken about how helpful mood monitoring can be and how to get started before, but it's more than just clearing your mind and getting thoughts off your chest that help. This will also help you to recognize patterns and the root causes of your anxiety: if a person is aware of an anxious thought pattern, they will start working on anxiety reduction strategies. We recommend you to keep a' thinking log' of thoughts that cause your anxiety (i.e., limbic reaction to perceived danger from their bodies). Many times we find that thoughts have a pattern. Everything can be a catalyst from the time of day to specific individuals. If a pattern has been established, the individual can then be proactive and prepare when these triggers are on the horizon.

Do you get worried by your boss calling you into her office? Recognize this instead, and start to question the feelings that make you nervous. Tell yourself, for example, that you have fulfilled all of your commitments and done nothing wrong (assuming that is true, that is). Challenge the thought-provoking fear by reminding yourself you haven't done something that would merit a negative discussion (again, assuming that's true).

Then come up with a "good outcome mindset" by saying to yourself that your boss may call you in to thank you. Although this exercise does not eliminate the fear, it will certainly help prevent you from being a nervous wreck. In other words, the pessimistic line of thought will slow down and not ultimately drive you to Panic-Ville.

For example, if you suffer from social anxiety or awkwardness, you can help recognize the types of scenarios that cause your anxiety by keeping a thinking journal like this. When you can paint a straightforward picture, methods to react positively to those situations are easier to find.

Final Words

Thank you again for purchasing this book!

We hope this book can help you.

The next step is for you to **join our email newsletter** to receive updates on any upcoming new book releases or promotions. You can sign-up for free, and as a bonus, you will also receive our "*7 Fitness Mistakes You Don't Know You're Making*" book! This bonus book breaks down many of the most common fitness mistakes and will demystify many of the complexities and science of getting into shape. Having all this fitness knowledge and science organized into an actionable step-by-step book will help you get started in the right direction in your fitness journey! To join our free email newsletter and grab your free book, please visit the link and signup: **www.effingopublishing.com/gift**

Finally, if you enjoyed this book, then we would like to ask you for a favor, would you be kind enough to leave a review for this book? It would be greatly appreciated! Thank you, and good luck on your journey!

About the Co-Authors

Our name is Alex & George Kaplo; we're both certified personal trainers from Montreal, Canada. We will start by saying we are not the biggest guys you will ever meet, and this has never really been our goal. We started working out to overcome our biggest insecurity when we were younger, which was our self-confidence. You may be going through some challenges right now, or you may simply want to get fit, and we can certainly relate.

We always kind were interested in the health & fitness

world and wanted to gain some muscle due to the numerous bullying in our teenage years. We figured we could do something about how our body looks like. This was the beginning of our transformation journey. We had no idea where to start, but we both just got started. We felt worried and afraid at times that other people would make fun of us for doing the exercises the wrong way. We always wished we had a friend to guide us and who could just show us the ropes.

After a lot of work, studying, and countless trials and errors. Some people began to notice how we were both getting more fit and how we were starting to form a keen interest in the topic. This led many friends and new faces to come to us and ask us for fitness advice. At first, it seemed odd when people asked us to help them get in shape. But what kept us going is when they started to see changes in their own body and told us it's the first time that they saw real results! From there, more people kept coming to us, and it made both of us realize after so much reading and studying in this field that it did help us, but it also allowed us to help others. To date, we have coached and trained numerous clients who have achieved some pretty amazing results.

Today, both of us own & operate this publishing business, where we bring passionate and expert authors to write about health and fitness topics. We also run an online fitness business, and we would love to connect with you by inviting you to visit the website on the following page and signing up for our e-mail newsletter (you will even get a free book).

Last but not least, if you are in the position we were once in and you want some guidance, don't hesitate and ask... I will be there to help you out!

Your coaches,

Alex &George Kaplo

Download another book for Free

We want to thank you for purchasing this book and offer you another book (just as long and valuable as this book), "Health & Fitness Mistakes You Don't Know You're Making," completely free.

Visit the link below to signup and receive it:

www.effingopublishing.com/gift

In this book, we will break down the most common health & fitness mistakes, you are probably committing right now, and will reveal how you can easily get in the best shape of your life!

In addition to this valuable gift, you will also have an opportunity to get our new books for free, enter giveaways, and receive other valuable emails from us. Again, visit the link to sign up:

www.effingopublishing.com/gift

Copyright 2019 by Effingo Publishing - All Rights Reserved.

This document by Effingo Publishing, owned by the A&G Direct Inc company, is geared towards providing exact and reliable information in regards to the topic and issue covered. The publication is sold with the idea that the publisher is not required to render accounting, officially permitted or otherwise qualified services. If advice is necessary, legal or professional, a practiced individual in the profession should be ordered.

From a Declaration of Principles which was accepted and approved equally by a Committee of the American Bar Association and a Committee of Publishers and Associations.

In no way is it legal to reproduce, duplicate, or transmit any part of this document in either electronic means or printed format. Recording of this publication is strictly prohibited, and any storage of this document is not allowed unless with written permission from the publisher. All rights reserved.

The information provided herein is stated to be truthful and consistent, in that any liability, in terms of inattention or otherwise, by any usage or abuse of any policies, processes, or directions contained within is the solitary and utter responsibility of the recipient reader. Under no circumstances will any legal responsibility or blame be held against the publisher for any reparation, damages, or monetary loss due to the information herein, either directly or indirectly.

The information herein is offered for informational purposes solely and is universal as so. The presentation of the information is without a contract or any type of guarantee assurance.

The trademarks that are used are without any consent, and the publication of the trademark is without permission or backing by the trademark owner. All trademarks and brands within this book are for clarifying purposes only and are owned by the owners themselves, not affiliated with this document.

For more great books, visit:

EffingoPublishing.com

www.ingramcontent.com/pod-product-compliance
Lightning Source LLC
Chambersburg PA
CBHW070930080526
44589CB00013B/1455